spot

HOLIDAYS

HANUKKAH

by Mari Schuh

AMICUS | AMICUS INK

menorah

dreidel

Look for these words and pictures as you read.

gold coins

donut

A candle is lit.
It's Hanukkah!

Hanukkah is often in December.
It's the Jewish festival of lights.
It's eight days long.

menorah

See the menorah?

The candles are lit.

They help count the eight days.

See the dreidel?

It spins.

It has four sides.

It's a fun game!

dreidel

gold coins

See the gold coins?

They are made of chocolate.

Kids get them as gifts.

donut

See the donut?

It's fried in oil.

Jelly is inside.

Yum!

People go to parties.
They go to temples.
They pray at home.

menorah

dreidel

Did you find?

gold coins

donut

Spot is published by Amicus and Amicus Ink
P.O. Box 1329, Mankato, MN 56002
www.amicuspublishing.us

Library of Congress Cataloging-in-Publication Data
Names: Schuh, Mari C., 1975- author.
Title: Hanukkah / by Mari Schuh.
Description: Mankato, Minnesota : Amicus/Amicus Ink,
  [2020] | Series: Spot holidays
Identifiers: LCCN 2018047348 (print) | LCCN 2018047942
  (ebook) | ISBN 9781681518442 (pdf) | ISBN 9781681518046
(library binding) | ISBN 9781681525327 (pbk.)
Subjects: LCSH: Hanukkah—Juvenile literature.
Classification: LCC BM695.H3 (ebook) | LCC BM695.H3 S3933
  2020 (print) | DDC 394.267—dc23
LC record available at https://lccn.loc.gov/2018047348

Printed in China

HC   10 9 8 7 6 5 4 3 2 1
PB   10 9 8 7 6 5 4 3 2 1

Alissa Thielges, editor
Deb Miner, series designer
Veronica Scott, book designer
Holly Young and Shane Freed,
   photo researchers

Photos by Getty/Jupiterimages cover,
16; iStock/traveler1116 1; Getty/Ariel
Skelley 3; Getty/Michael Cogliantry
4–5; iStock/belchonock 6–7; Getty/
jessicanelson 8–9; Shutterstock/Derek
Hatfield 10–11; iStock/yula 12–13;
iStock/kali9 14–15

HANUKKAH